MAKING MY PEACE

POEMS

by Michael L. Newell

ACKNOWLEDGEMENTS

Many of these poems (sometimes in a different form) have previously appeared in the following periodicals, to whose editors grateful acknowledgement is made: *Bellowing Ark*; *Culture Counter*; *Current*; *The Iconoclast*; *Inwood Indiana Press: Tracks*; *Jerry Jazz Musician*; *Section 8 Magazine*; *Ship of Fools*; *Verse-Virtual.*

I would like to tip my cap to the following editors who have treated my work kindly over the years and been most supportive in other ways as well: Robert R. Ward, Jerry Austin, Phil Wagner, Jack Hart, Don Wentworth, Firestone Feinberg, and Joe Maita.

I would also like to thank the following folk for their kindness to my work over a span of many years and for their generous friendship: Anna and Michael Citrino, David Ellenstein, Robert Fox, Joseph Glaser, Stellasue Lee, Michael Minassian, Lawrence Noel, Ed Ruzicka, and Robert Wexelblatt.

Cover Photo: *Winter* by Wendy Keller

Author Photo: Michael Citrino

Table of Contents

Table of Contents (page two)

Table of Contents (page three)

Table of Contents (page four)

This book of poems is dedicated to the teachers (now all departed) who did the most to shape me in useful ways as a thinker, writer, teacher, actor, director, and poet. I think of them almost daily. This is my salute to Robert Ellenstein, Mary Jane Evans, Donald Salper, and Benjamin Saltman. Blessings on them, one and all.

MAKING MY PEACE

poems by

Michael L. Newell

"The game enforces smirks; but we have seen
The moon in lonely alleys make
a grail of laughter of an empty ash can..."

--Hart Crane ("Chaplinesque")

AN OLD MAN CELEBRATES HIS COMPANION

Your hair adrift in a spring breeze
carries me back through decades, waves
as you jog forest paths, ages, changes
color from auburn to grey over years,
as time has us both in its grasp, re-coloring
hair, filling joints with arthritis, mutating

the way we once soared together into
gimpy limping relics of another time, and yet,
and yet, and yet, behind those lines,
I see even today the wild grin of youth,
the exuberant laughter that came unbidden
and was inexhaustible, the gracious

smile and caress that forgave all and turned
difficult times into sagas of hope, and no,
you have never abandoned our journey
together no matter how often we slipped and fell,
and for all these things and many more than I can
enumerate, I sing a song of love and possibility.

THE PAST IS EVER WITH US

Faces shine from deep within my mind
where all I treasure from a lengthening past
can still be found, as memory's sunlight splays
in certain ways across long-forgotten landscapes,
and suddenly there they are, all the lads, lasses,
and parents passed away during my early days,
faces that shine like newly minted coins
tossed into a clear pool smiling up at me --
the lad slowly dying of leukemia, yet still playing
on a school's summer softball team; the mother
of my best friend, wanly smiling, as she gave us
wonderful baked goods while only weeks

from passing on from brain cancer; the classmate's
wee bairn of a brother run over by a truck
backing up in a parking lot next to a small
community store, his blood baked into
asphalt by a hot summer North Carolina sun, blood
we would stare at every time we visited the store;
the college classmate who, on his first film job,
died in a plane crash over the Santa Monica mountains
a few hours after leaving his supportive
(yet somewhat jealous) classmates to board
the plane carrying him to his disappearance
from our lives, his palpable joy mutated into

our continuing grief, leavened by stories
we would tell of him as aspiring actor,
awkward wooer of one lass or another,
and acts of generosity largely unacknowledged;
these eidolons and many others seem to fill
my inner vision far more often as I stumble
toward my own finish line -- the past seems
richer and more alive than what lies ahead,
and I ache for all I have done, and for all I haven't,
and I sing songs (when alone) of life's beauty,
its losses, its surprises, its paths known and unknown;
and the older I grow, the more the past rises

up around me, a rich landscape still not fully understood,
not fully accepted, yet always whispering
a strange music that baffles yet nourishes me.

UNSOUGHT GIFTS

Otter on his back underwater
swiftly flows down creek's current,
a playful living poem embodying
joy, wild freedom, physical communion

with water and all that lives within it;
I watch from nearby bridge where I stand
in a downpour, half-blinded by rain
streaming down my glasses, yet I am

happier than I have been in months
as I discover the otter passing a heron
poised on a log, realize telephone wires
strung over the bridge are filled with small

songbirds twittering, chirping, and clinging
to wires in face of steady wind and downpour,
realize I am soaked, but I do not want to leave.
A passing car sprays me thoroughly as it

plows through multiple puddles. I find myself
laughing, face tilted back to embrace
all the sky holds for me, hold tightly
to my tweed cap so it won't sail into the creek,

and sing an old folk song, "Didn't it rain,
Children, talk about rain all night long."
I wave at a passing car filled with children
who wave back. In the distance I see deer

head into trees and heavy brush. My recent
depression has vanished. So have
otter and heron, but in my memory
they lift me high above all that I can see.

TIME TIME TIME

Seated on a pier in a river's inlet
as evening falls, an old man sips
Pouilly-Fuisse while mist seeps
across landscape, and loons
across the river serenade night,

one another, and the old chap
who dreams of a girl fifty years
in the past who floated down
this river in a canoe with him,
a minor journey filled with visions

detailing all they might share
over the years looming before them.
The haunting cries of the loons,
an owl circling nearby woods,
and distant call of a coyote fill

the old man with a sense of all
he has lost over decades between
canoe ride and the present.
Wine swirls in its glass, creates
eddies of memory in man's mind, as he

dreams of all that has been
and all that has not. He wonders
about the girl, whether she still
lives, whether she has done better
than he has in the years from

the canoe until now. He struggles
to his feet, blesses the river
with an offering of what wine
remains in the bottle, imagines
his thoughts can embrace the night

and thanks the universe for river,
mist, barely visible stars
and moon, the girl still alive in his mind,
and slowly hobbles off into the night
on a slow path home where silence awaits.

AFTERMATH OF THEATRE PERFORMANCES

years ago I was an actor
I loved the stage
often the only time I was at peace
was onstage

after abandoning the theatre
or being abandoned by it
I was never quite sure
I visited some of the stages

where I had trod the boards
always when no one was around
I would stand in silence
in audience or onstage and listen

after a time voices would whisper
at first I would not know them
then I would recognize speech patterns know
voices and imagine forgotten figures rising before me

the empty stage would fill with shapes of sets and figures
moving on and off stage and I would know
many of these figures and at times witness
myself a ghost in heated exchanges with other eidolons

I could neither move nor speak join the world of apparitions
or abandon them I could merely listen and watch
at times I discovered mirth and silently laughed
at other times I was moved to tears

inevitably someone would enter and the world would vanish
I would be asked to leave which I would quickly do head down
to hide tears offering no explanation realizing
my experience was as close to sacred as I was capable of knowing

many of those actors have departed and exist only in memory
many of those stages are gone some replaced some not
yet actors theatres productions here or vanished enrich
my dreams my memory my daily life as little else can

and I celebrate what is still present remember what is lost and sing
a poet's praise for men and women who create magical worlds
make dreams and acts of imagination corporeal and kinetic
and dare to cut veins to paint imaginary landscapes

AN ACTRESS

In the hallway before the performance,
she could barely whisper in response
to questions. Her head was bowed as if

in prayer, and her walk clumsy as
a newborn colt. Her dark hair absorbed
the overhead lights, reflecting nothing.

When she appeared onstage, she was
blinding energy, all light and sound;
everyone and every thing on stage

disappeared, and she stood alone amidst
many. The audience laughed, stared,
sucked in its breath in dismay, and released

it joyfully, in response to each action
and line she liberated into the world
of the play. Then it was over, everyone

feeling a sudden loss. What had just
happened? What had changed?
The curtain call was swift, perfunctory.

In hallway outside the stage, she whispered
in response to praise showered from every
side, and apologetically entered dressing room,

head down, hair draping face from view, save
for one haunted eye seeking shelter, and
shoulders hunched as though avoiding a blow.

EMPTY THEATRES

I often have walked into empty theatres.
I have sat on bare stages and listened.
Soon, if there are no interruptions,
the air begins to murmur.

I have sat on bare stages and listened.
Try it some time if you dare.
The air begins to murmur.
Your bones will clack a rhythm in response.

Try it some time if you dare.
Every empty theatre has a hidden life.
Your bones will clack a rhythm in response.
Don't go there if you hate the theatre.

Every empty theatre has a hidden life.
It embraces all who love imagination, heart, and wit.
Don't go there if you hate the theatre.
It will leave you deaf and blind if you lack love.

It embraces all who love imagination, heart, and wit--
soon, if there are no interruptions.
It will leave you deaf and blind if you lack love.
I often have walked into empty theatres.

AN OLD ACTOR, AN ABANDONED THEATRE

The stage lies bare and ruined,
No sets, no actors, no dreams.
Yet something won't know its end.

There are whisperers who blend
Their voices into pale streams.
The stage lies bare and ruined.

In the moonlight figures wend
Their ways over fallen beams.
Here something won't know its end.

He thinks he sees an old friend
Who first played here in his teens.
The stage lies bare and ruined.

All through the ruins, the wind
Sends a deep-throated keening.
Here something won't know its end.

Hist, hist, more voices tune in:
Who are these, what is their theme?
The stage lies bare and ruined,
Yet something won't know its end.

AFTER THE CURTAIN CALL

applause dims
the house empties
only a ghost light

hints at what took place
mere minutes before
the sighing air parts

to permit the final actor his trek
to the door and a hesitant
disappearance into darkness

a murmur fills the emptiness
as though lives were being reenacted
in someone's memory

QUEST

(for David Ellenstein, Jonathan McMurtry, and John Herzog)

Slipping from shadow to light and back,
an actor seeks meaning

in word, gesture, tilt of head, glance, smile, smirk,
scowl, unpacking of heart, and unleashing of voice;

this journey will take a lifetime
of two and three hour segments.

When an actor dies, his ashes
will bless the earth to the tenth generation.

His ghost will blend with shadows of a hundred
theatres he has known and inhabited.

EVENING THEATRE

suspended deep within creek
full moon resplendent
fish swim through its golden presence
a chalice rippling in underwater silence

loons nesting in hardstem bulrushes
fill night with haunting calls soaring
in every direction dispensing
lovely melancholy never forgotten

wind rises swaying tree plant bush
and slides its chill caress down neck
onto back and sends me slowly ambling
home as leaves blow down street

in slow motion ballet defined by lift fall
swirl float into marriage of air and earth

SEATED ON CHAIR OUTSIDE FRONT DOOR

windblown dark clouds sweep
across midnight firmament
patches of clear sky reveal sprinkling
of stars whose presence always

evokes joy and then
light breaks through
a dark squadron of clouds
which slowly parts to reveal

a full yellow moon
that warms the night
and lifts me in surprise
to my feet

SLIPPING INTO DARKNESS

creek curves
into oncoming twilight
old man in rowboat
arms wide
embraces night
last embers of daylight
set his hair aflame
and breeze-blown water
sings him on his way

GOING HOME

truant old man lost
in remnants of gloaming
fades into woodland
next to river

THE VISITOR

as I lounge in the dark
the moon visits my teacup
floats as though a water craft
meant to ferry me through dreams
and I feel song welling up full-throated
and I give voice to music unknown to me
and night sky swirls and whirls and I am a child again
and in my private world all is reborn young and beautiful
ah let us dance to the music dance to the music now and forever dance

SIMPLE SONG

birdsong birdsong birdsong
fills morning with delight
so I sing of spring
as birds take flight

in all directions
and music fills the land
all day long and joy
sets right all that is wrong

RITES

dancing and singing
in icy rain: morning
ablutions for old man

neighbors shake their heads
crow squawks
wind swirls tree bush and sleet

the ancient spreads his arms
lifts face to sky and carols
the hills with his broken voice

ONE MIDNIGHT IN LA PAZ

adrift in beauty and wonder

lost in a midnight Andean sky
my mind flies through time and space

thought and imagination interwoven

and everywhere and everything
sings of astonishment more astonishment

and possibility possibility possibility

THE MUSICIAN BEGINS

A note, then another, floats
upon the breath of the man
giving life to the shakuhachi,

rises into a late spring
afternoon where wind has stilled,
rain has drifted into the past,

and all movement seems suspended
save for the slow drift of breath
and fingers gliding in creation

over the flute that holds all sorrow
in the loose grasp of hope, joy,
and the wild surmise of possibility.

Night approaches, but even as day
recedes, the listener feels a smile
grow and linger as notes rise and fall.

FINDING A PATH

Beyond a harsh freezing wind,
across creek and field

filled with bending reeds,
are hills rising green clad

with fir trees into a distance
where shelter from wind

and rain might be found,
along with the possibility

of an unknowable future
stretching past vision's limits.

POTENTIAL

beauty lies coiled in stillness
in silence

in the moment before
a breath is taken

in a flickering decision
to waltz tango or paso doble

the moment before decides
shape and scope and possibility

MURMURING RAIN

Long rainy afternoon wraps lad in window
in a blanket of silence as his eyes track
flights of small birds winging through wet

skies in search of whatever shelter they
can find; take me with you, he whispers,
take me to the ends of the earth; the birds

vanish into a setting sun, the boy
slips into dreamless sleep, and the rain
continues its gently soothing susurration.

(RE)DISCOVERY

it is only in silence we hear
those murmurs of the heart
which sing of all our interred

dreams lost longings shreds
of desires which once filled
our hours with hope

turn off the radio remove
the iPod unplug the computer
television and DVD open

the curtains window and doors
even   dare I whisper it   step outside
walk silent night streets where only

the moon wind and an occasional
cat or dog keep us company
rediscover the panoply of stars

tossed in wild abandon above
listen for wings beating animal cries
whispers from bedrooms gliding past

let time become glistening drops
of water strung from infinite string
where we slip freely forth and back

A HARVEST

The moon pours forth
a golden stream.

We stand in a meadow
in still air,

bathing in light
while listening to cricket hum

and catching glimpses of an owl
trawling nearby woods and fields.

At times such as this, even stone
seems ready to burst into bloom.

SEEKING TRANQUILLITY

the rain was persistent--like blues in the heart
of one who listens to the breath of the universe

as it whispers in his ear   all can be clear   all can
be felt   all can be heard   all can be known

bury all you own   walk away from the city   seek
desert forest mountain ocean river stream   seek silence

seek birdsong   seek the quiet moment before your lover
begins the dance of heat and passion that culminates in ashes

to baptize your life   wear her touch as the softest of garments
to warm you when the winds of life would freeze all they touch   stop

listen   all awaits whoever would embrace silence   the heart   and what
is more than   vaster than   anything man can create   right this moment

slip into time's stream   accept the night   the infinite floating
of mind and heart   do you hear it   the whisper filling time and space

SCANT COMFORT

years and miles roll past
I settle
into a couch's cushions

read poems by other
wanderers   Li Po
Tu Fu   Basho   Robert Sund

closing the books
I dream of twenty friends
unseen for years

where are the fields
of boyhood   vanished
into the dusty corridors

of memory   where are
the guides who led me
to the hills overlooking the world

and nudged me out onto
my long journey   looking back
only tree lined slopes limned

by storm clouds   each step
is a mile further away from the past
across an ocean one or two friends

send greetings through e-mail's semaphore
and my father awaits the long night
with stoic grace

while my mother cradles
in her wrinkled hands the gifts
and griefs of a lifetime

sooner or later we all
are alone   unknown
poetry a scant comfort

CONSIDER

one day soon you will slide into
welcoming soil where you will
turn into dust which will ride
the long wind toward the endless night
which waits stoically for all existence
to rejoin its uncaring blindness

meanwhile there are trees to plant
children who need songs sung to them
lovers to join in their brief frolics
the aged who value reminders they still live
and the butterfly soaring above the backyard
before vanishing vanishing vanishing

seldom has poached teriyaki salmon
tasted so good as tonight gazing
at storm tossed branches while listening
to Albinoni oboe concerti navigated
by Heinz Holliger as rain glides in long
rivulets down unwashed windowpanes

consider each day and night left you consider
how each moment may be transfigured

DUET

the silence awaits

he waits
in silence

the door is cracked open
waiting for the swing
outward

he rocks
he rocks
he rocks
he rocks

she slips an arm
round him
and breathes in rhythm
with his faltering breaths
wanting to share to the last

De Profundis Clamavi ad te, Domine
Out of the depths I have cried to you, Lord
silence echoes all night
silence resounds
filled by failing breath
and a slow rocking…

TO FATHOM AND ENJOY

"The brevity of wit" is but metaphor
for a necessity to cram meaning into life's

too short, often redundant, frequently saccharine,
few pages of clumsy events, empty dialogue, and random relationships.

Who would not, if he could, speak concisely,
act with precise abandon, and cultivate only

those friendships whose fields yielded clear thought,
generous acts, and the passionate flowers of self-sacrifice

and knowledge of the heart? "Wit" is but succinct
rendering of the need to fathom and enjoy.

FACE TO FACE IN THE TWILIGHT

Night cools slowly as rage sheds its fiery skin.
A slow breeze wraps itself round me. It carries
voices from thousands of miles away, voices last
heard decades ago. Some conversations never end;
some arguments appear again and again--still
no conclusion, no relief from fugues of betrayal
and grief. A thousand times reproached; a thousand
times forgiven. Perhaps this breeze will carry
away today's arguments, yesterday's fury--all
of memory's caches emptied into time's swift waters,
the holy waters of healing. Its current sweeps
us into a future we can (we tell ourselves) shape
into a world where anger is unknown, words never
are used as daggers. This we tell ourselves; we tell
ourselves; I tell myself. Again the wind whispers of the past.
Who arises out of the fog: lover, friend, enemy, myself?

DINNER WITH THE CITRINOS

Is that laughter   no by God   that is a geyser
of silvery sound erupting into space above
our heads before drenching one and all
with joyful abandon   damn that Anna   she

just won't let anyone be sad   and who is that
bearded dude on the other side of the table
unleashing verbal riffs like some sort of freeform
spoken blues   conversation as jazz   what a concept

I think of a line I once read comparing art to children
making mud pies which they recommend to one another's
sympathetic consideration   this meal meets (no pun intended)

that standard   life as mud pies tossed gleefully in the air to see
who can catch them and then rework them into new shapes
all we need are jump ropes to leap above while tossing the pies

DE GUSTIBUS NON DISPUTANDUM EST

the heart invests eyes
with a gift of vision

which sees the desired
rather than the real

that chin is not a pier
where boats tie up

it is a charming sign
of a loved one's determination

those ears aren't satellite dishes
for a neighborhood's television sets

they are an amusing flaw which gives
humanity to an otherwise perfect face

and that stomach which blocks
vision of the feet

is actually a sign that its owner
is rooted in the real world

strange others are too blind
to see these truths

A DIGGER'S PRAYER

Into the loam of phoneme and morpheme,
I thrust my pen, bleed dreams, fears, hopes,
and all the griefs I have rooted out of my mind
and heart to lay as fertilizer, and search

for signs of syntax vines to signify my life
and all the lives of those for whom I care,
even those I have never met who nonetheless
have shaped my understanding of life and death.

May I discover buried in the animal sounds
we so carelessly utter, joinings that wed us all
each to the other, throughout our short

and oft-times bitter histories. Let this produce
provide sustenance for us all, and these sounds,
though unrecognized, resound through generations.

A CACOPHONY OF LADS

they scramble
through field and wood

across brook and fen
follow chimes on the wind

scent blackberry
and honeysuckle

roar with the laughter
of ramblers who move

without rule or fetter
who know the moon's

hiding place who want
only myths originated

by the group who insist
day and night co-exist

inside one another and peer
out through the eyes

of all living things
their voices fill forest

meadow hill abandoned
railroad cars and my dreams

my dreams my
long running dreams

A FADING OF SONG

the tatters of a day bleed through a window
into a living room where an old man rocks
and hums old ballads sung to him by his mother

six or more decades before the words
no longer matter they are a mantra against
the silence which cloaks the room the pictures

full of the old man's dead the dust which hangs
in the air like unspoken words waiting
for the right moment to unleash themselves

upon the unwary the helpless the lost
one fading photo of a smiling young woman
holding a rose in her left hand and a vase

in her right sits on a table next to the rocker
every so often his eyes stray to her and the tune
shifts to Amazing Grace and the voice

strengthens for a few bars before crumbling
into fragments of half-remembered songs
an old hound softly whines in its sleep and the day

deepens to night the old man begins to snore
the curtains lift and fall and a soft rain washes the air
a phone rings and rings and falls silent

A FAREWELL NOTE

Sun drenched streets,
air laden with bird song,
trees in luxuriant bloom,

these mean nothing
when the news comes:
an old friend, unseen for years,

has been planted beneath
flower, grass, and tree
so long loved and cultivated.

The friend, once cherished, is now
food for all. It would be
easy to resent the bird caterwauling

from a nearby building. It would be
convenient to curse the plant taking
root in what was once flesh and blood.

The friend's voice murmurs in my head:
we are all one; we nourish what nourishes
us. Celebrate life. Accept that we too

will one day decay into food
for new life. I hear and douse
my resentment, yet it will be some time

before bird song, blossom, honeysuckle's
fragrance wafted on a warm spring wind,
will bring anything but regret.

The moon at my midnight window strikes
the right note--reflected beauty left behind
after sunset/regret and salvation through memory.

A HYMN AT PARTING

The rivers of the heart fill with grief
for all who shared word and song
and the nourishing bread of laughter with us,
who now are vanished into the void where we
all stare, a nothingness one slight step away.
Their voices whisper in leaf-breeze, their mirth
bubbles in brook, stream, and tumbling breakers;
in summer sunshine, their touch lightly strokes
the back of the neck, caresses hair and beard.
Wait brother. Stay, sister. We come. Soon we come.
Night spreads its sable cloak. We dream of our future.

A TIME FOR RIPENING

the year swings round
the day grows a morning and an evening

the sun's pale radiance ripens to gold
wheat and corn rain upon the earth

lads and lasses pursue the light
even unto night's waterfall of moon and stars

fireflies anoint the night no one retires
until well past the hour of exhaustion

dawn lifts one and all from bed cot and cradle
sunflowers lifting faces toward the light

the young look toward one another with anticipation
the old rock with the rhythm of blown stalks

they see all that happens and nod approval
dream of wind in their hair sun kneading flesh and bone

the young lengthen toward marriage and children
the parchment skin of the old is candlelit from within

A JUBILATION

to dance on a note
an angel balanced
on the head of a pin

to swim oceans
with a dolphin's
ease and grace

to soar with an
eagle's power
and serene balance

ah Ludwig ah Wolfgang
ah JSB how did you do
the feats you did

create such beauty
while buried in life's
mundane litter

forests grow rivers flow
mountains loom and valleys
curve down and far far away

your mighty seas of sound
fill the landscape of our lives
with the same wonder and hope

how did you do
the things you did how
do we ever repay you

every breeze every flower
every wild stream's power
lives on in your currents

A SPRING TUNE

A chortle of children, lads and lasses,
flocks across railroad tracks
and country roads, a dozen or so
at mirth in a brazen spring world.

Their hands, a field
of windmills, carve the bee-laden
spoor-filled bird-blessed air
into sheaves of golden laughter.

All afternoon they trek
the fields and hills rolling round
the town in a shouted search for the liquor
of merriment, the lilted melody

of new beginnings, the tentative first
steps of the long waltz of courtship.

A TRUE BELIEVER

the rooms and halls were filled
with young and old cursing
the spring snowstorm

but one lad walked out into
the swirling white certain
a miracle was visiting the city

that polar bears walruses seals reindeer
Inuits and Laplanders would appear
that chocolate would grow on trees

that gargoyles would take flight
that his dead grandfather would step from
out the white cloud enfolding earth and sky

in his eager ears the wind
was an orchestra playing a tone poem
about possibility hope and imagination

indifferent to time or cold
the lad meditated on the gifts
that might be found in his cathedral

A LOVESONG

all wind the night
all rain the day
all fight her love
all lust his play

no when she said
what how he bled
where why she asked
then now he gasped

world which her whisper
this this his answer
spun light she moaned
sweet sleep he groaned

collapse into deep
slumber through mourn
dawn sings him gone
sway dusk her song

A SERENADE

her sleepy smile
sunset's last rays
deepening into
warm shadows

her dark hair upon a cream pillowcase
the milky way on a moonless night

wind and rain on
the window panes
chamber music lilting
a heart's melody and rhythm
may this night never end may this
moment flower into a lifetime

****

such beauty unrehearsed wounds
all who witness   it will be lost
it can never be regained
memory wraps it in silk

now and again take it out and look at
fading loveliness until only dust remains

murmured the autumn breeze
in the yellowing trees
whispered the owl's wings
ghosting through the night

A TUNE FOR ANTHONY

the lad is transfixed by lass after lass offers
his heart on waterford crystal for approval
again and again he receives smiles and gracious
refusal still he holds up his gift for any

willing to receive it into safekeeping
he lilts a tune of roses and shamrocks
his accent the purest sylvan honey
all are charmed but none walk off with him

to watch a sunset or stroll a field
yet still he turns to one then another
and proffers all that he is all that he will be
may the wind spin him round to face

a direction where one appears who sees
his gift for the courageous act it is
who accepts it in exchange for her heart
who moves with him through wood and city street

ADRIFT ON THE RIVER OF NIGHT

the orchestral roar of crickets
fills night's recesses

I abandon my body to move
through forests of fireflies

stars gleam with the warmth
of precious stones set on black velvet

in this space alone with wonder
I discover a path back to boyhood

where the night sky meant the future
would bring unknown marvels

where every constellation held a story
and every adult was a magician who could

lead treks to places never before visited
when I rejoin my body my clothes

are heavy with dew and the silence
is a blanket to wear on the journey

back home to four walls a roof
and the balance sheet of daily life

looking out the bedroom window an owl
a dangerous thought cloaked

in symmetry's beauty
drifts through a shaft of moonlight

AN APPARITION

Is that a lost friend's voice at my shoulder
as I walk in leisurely fashion the streets
of Tallinn? No, it is the wind

within which sounds a day we walked
together down a lonely beach where
waves raged and old men muttered

to themselves and poked about
in the sand with metal detectors
while we held hands and imagined

a future that never came. We were
happy in the mist and at peace
with one another. I look around

and see young couples hand in hand
laughing in the wintry wind and scooting
rapidly over ice patches and pockets

of snow. May they grow old with joy
intact, friendship undamaged, and dreams
grown to fruition, at peace in an arbor of children.

Wherever you have wandered off to, may your
nights be full of comfort and your days at ease
in sunlight, cool breeze, and laughter's warmth.

AN INVITATION TO LIFE

Where has she gone, the girl
who exchanged glances with you
across classrooms, cafeteria,
passing in hallways, who always seemed

about to speak--so you remained
mute and thus you would pass
each other, a relationship in a state
of perpetual possibility never realized.

Did she finally speak or did someone
speak to her? Do they have a house
with three or four children, two mortgages,
doctor bills, dentist bills, clothing and grocery bills?

Do they no longer see the person they met
when first they extended hands each to each?
When the wind blows, do they imagine
wings, a far destination, and a new partner?

I would like to think when they come
to the end of a bad day they look up,
see one who heals life's bruises and contusions,
that smile and touch remain an invitation to life.

BEARINGS

A step towards tomorrow,
the Irish lad hugging the Polish lass
next to their lockers in the school corridor.

The wind tugging my neck
suggests a direction unconsidered
which now seems inevitable.

Rain pelting a street drives
people into doorways with unexpected
conversational consequences.

A random autumn leaf sails for blocks,
an odyssey of sorts; without question
we follow, oddly eager, alert to possibility.

BEING DISCREET WE LEAVE THEM HERE

stars moon wind
three that fill
a long night

she he the singing
bedroom where light and
wind spill through window

breakfast table silence glance gesture
and touch the only language
sun's promise drapes the room

DOING THE BANQUET

slide over here slip your hand in mine no crime
doing time together on the couch on the floor
rolling round the table move the casserole honey
we'll make our own kind of dinner if you know (I know)
what you mean the wine (oh yeah) can stay (mm hm)
and where should the baked beans go (I've got a suggestion)
oh you're nasty (heh heh heh) gravy anyone (I've got
another idea) oh stop   or maybe not   do you think perhaps
this is getting out of control (oh I hope so) you're incorrigible
(one of my best traits according to my last dinner companion)
I thought that was me (oh I hope so) you're repeating yourself
(a little repetition never hurt anyone--at least not in this position)
try a little harder (mm an old song lyric never hurt anyone)
when are the children due home (forget the children   let's finish
at least one meal without being concerned about them) I'm not
concerned I'm worried   they might walk in and nothing would be
worse than their catching parents in the middle of a feast (oh you talk
so dirty   I just love it) forget the talk let's just chow down
(I prefer to think we are slip sliding away) shhh it's crying time again...

WITHOUT AND WITHIN

slanting sheets of rain lash house
tree bush and street

a switch is thrown
stillness envelops neighborhood

light suffuses windows summoning
all inside onto porch and lawn

a sudden clarity all color intensifies
faces lit from within are transparent

each thought each feeling butterflies
floating through crystalline air

never have we loved so much
never have we known others so well

clouds recover the day we stumble
back indoors uncertain what we have witnessed

all afternoon we glance longingly over shoulders
searching for what has vanished

the wind's aria swells an ocean of air and sound
releasing a world of hope sorrow longing loss

we rock through the evening in old wooden chairs
and wait for forests to reclaim the land

what is that keening through wall cracks
what scratches at the door

A BIOGRAPHICAL NOTE

one day I was young and dancing in the wind
when that old gypsy time swept me up
in her voluminous arms and carried me
down more roads than I imagined possible

it was a dream of many years it was a dance
with no name and no clear destination
it was a poem whose words were a jumble
a joy a fantastic swirl of color and sound

and I awoke by the side of a road
and found myself old tired dazed
and disappointed to be discarded
by the colorful gypsy who had left me here

now I wait for the sound of the drums
which will march me off to the unknown
the skirling pipes which will lift me from this place
and the fiddle which will keen over and bless me

Kigali, Rwanda, October 2012

AGAIN THE BIRD SINGS

My daily early morning walk to school fills
with bird song from a bird unseen and unknown
whose sound is like three deep strikes on a gong,
the final note containing an echo inside an outer ring
of ever deepening and haunting sound;

one imagines a powerful heart contained against
its will, willing listeners to seek it out and free it;
the sky is clear, breeze-blown trees wave gently,
the dirt road is tranquil, the few walkers at peace,
but the bird cries out again and again;

always it utters this pattern in passionate repetition,
each utterance louder than the previous one,
each sound expanding wide, the final sound
once again containing an interior echo inside
the magnificent sound which cries for freedom;

the song haunts me all day, all week; on a day
when the song is not heard, I feel a loss; the singer
sings for each of us caught in a pattern we can not escape,
patterns which may provide meaning and paths through life,
but which limit our steps, our thoughts, our hopes

until we sing in conversation or letters or poems of what
we can not do, what will never be seen or known,
yet our songs carry beauty and power in their laments,
and the same is true of the unseen bird known only
through its three note lament which lightens my step,

an irony -- beauty rising from a creature I imagine
imprisoned; the bird, of course, may be free,
the prison exist solely in my imagination,
the song mere instinct, the images conjured
in my mind more indicative of listener

than of creature hidden in nearby trees or bushes;
bird song, poetry, conversation--are all conjurations,
dreams, figments of the imagination? Am I haunted
by the bird or my own longings and limitations?
I question whether beauty exists. Then again the bird sings.

(August 21, 2012, Kigali, Rwanda)

ALWAYS THE RAIN AND WIND

always the rain the wind
and I alone
in the rain and wind

on some muddy dirt road or
side path to nowhere
yet everywhere

are signs of others
that dot the journey
and summon memories

of elsewhere and elsewhen
times that satisfied or baffled
or amused or terrified

or rewarded the hours spent
before traveling on in search
of a future which yet contains

the past a search always
different and the same
will this stop

inevitably
but not until life
ceases

deceases
releases
the mind caught in wander and wonder

until then there is
the rain the wind and I
alone

in pursuit of something
perhaps nothing   who knows
the rain?   the wind?   not I

Kigali, Rwanda, January 2013

ALLELUIA

Rivers of color flood the sky,
usher in bird song, as windows open,
and the first people tentatively slip
out their doors into a new day
where hope, always welcome hope,
entices movement into life.

Stillness acquires motion,
motion achieves form and direction,
life blooms, night retreats,
and a day discovers what it will be.
I slip into the stream moving toward
the known and unknown,

and rejoice in another day,
one more chance to get it right.

Kigali, Rwanda, March 2014

ALL LIFE IS ARCHAIC

Along a country road, telephone wires carried
thousands of voices seeking others who were

far removed. Lives were altered and each
who spoke was never the same again.

Wind accompanied them on their long journey.
Birds rose from trees in witness. Scarecrows

stood silent, mouths agape. Rain and snow fell, time
swept past, crops grew, were harvested, and planted

once again, and still the voices flowed past, strangers
to the world which hosted them, unaware that other

voices had streamed through those fields
and woods. Today, however, the wires are archaic,

the voices travel other routes, and the rural world
which hosted those travelers disintegrates, as all

things must, as the voices and the owners of the voices
must, as the writer of these words must, as the sun

which warms the fields, forests, rivers, and streams must,
as the galaxy and universe must; yet still voices

travel vast distances through constantly changing means
to reach other voices, and writers continue to write,

thinkers to think, and lovers to love, and all is archaic,
as soon as it is said or done or thought, yet still we strive.

Kigali, Rwanda, November 2011

ADRIFT ONCE AGAIN

Lost again on winding dirt roads, I am a stranger
immediately identifiable by skin color (and partially by age),
in a land where all are black and few are old
(due to the not so distant genocide).
In the middle of this drifting wandering

journey through farm fields deep in valleys
(in the center of a large city), where shanties
are clumped in groups constructed from mud bricks
or other cheap materials, structures which
are homes and small shops, I hear music,

choral, a cappella, multi-harmonic,
vigorous, ecstatic, and come round
a twisting bend in a road deeply
pocked by rains and occasional
heavy motor vehicles to find a Catholic Church,

lovingly constructed and well-kept.
It is humble, neither large, nor grandiose
in color or shape or materials, but filled
with a passion I would associate with
holy roller churches in the American South.

A family is entering as I pass, and they call
to me, "Muzungu Muzungu." In broken English
(though why they would assume I speak English
instead of French, I don't know), they invite me
to enter the church. Being a devout agnostic,

I smile, politely decline, and wander off
in search of a landmark I recognize, or a face
who knows me and can point me home.
This is the story of my life, lost and needing
the goodwill of strangers who are separated

from me by age, language, race, and religion.
As often is the case, two men recognize me,
although I don't know them, but they know
where I live, figure out I am lost, walk me
partway home, pat me on my back and trust

I will make it the rest of the way. And I do.
I ask myself, as I enter the final few yards
of my two hour walk, are all the things
I experience life or the metaphor for a life
which is still waiting to happen. And I laugh.

Kigali, Rwanda, January 2012

A TIP OF THE HAT

Face in palm, eyes shut, I stare
into blackness, imagine
taking a step into nothingness,
calm and welcoming, an end
to continuous struggle with the thousand
cuts and bruises of everyday life,
the constant search for quiet and peace
in a world of grating, often cruel noise,

when I hear a tapping on the window
behind me and glance around to see
a small songbird trying to find his way
through the pane of glass; the small creature
flies repeatedly into the window, chirps,
hops to a nearby branch and repeats
his collision with the man made obstacle,
flying away only when I stand and walk

close to the window; I sit down and slide again
into my deep funk only to hear tapping at the window
loudly resume; I look behind me to see the bird
hop anew onto the same nearby branch and fly
into the window repeatedly, wings wildly aflutter
until the creature settles on the window sill
and resumes tapping on the window with his beak;
when I walk over to the window, the bird flies

off to a tree across the street; I settle into a chair,
take a deep breath, wonder what I can do
to find the energy to overcome my gloom,
and hear tap tap tap on the window; I wheel around
and little dude is back again trying to find his way
into my darkened room; yet again I move toward
the window and the bird flies away once more;
from a nearby tree the creature starts to sing, full-throated

and passionate in a way I seldom am about anything
these days; as I listen to the concert, I grow aware
that a number of birds are singing up and down
the street, girls in the yard next door are jumping rope
to chants in Kinyarwanda, small lads are chasing
tires that they are rolling up and down hill with
small sticks; a young couple wanders leisurely up
the street finding every possible reason to laugh,

bump hips, touch one another on the arm;
and an old cripple that I know (he was a polio
victim many years ago) lurches down the hill
and suddenly looks up at me with a smile
which erupts like a bright sun bursting through
dark threatening clouds and lifts both his arms
over his head and waves open palms in
a typical Rwandan greeting; I tip my cap to him

and he moves on down the street laughing;
I look around and realize this dark day has grown
more interesting; the papers piled on my desk
to grade no longer seem like an exercise
in futility, the hours of work ahead are promising;
I read the first essay and discover it is not only
intelligent, but worth reading even if it were not
an assignment; I hear a tapping; the little fellow

has returned; he has resumed his assault on
my window; I slowly walk over; as soon as I am
close enough for him to see, the small fellow flies off;
earlier he annoyed me; now I forgive him;
whatever his confusion, he has guided me back
into life; I marvel at his determination, however
ill-advised it may be, and envy his tenacity; silently
I thank this stranger for re-engaging me with life.

April 2013, Kigali, Rwanda

A STORM AND THE HEART

(for David Ellenstein, Joseph Glaser, and Lawrence Noel)

Clouds feathered the sky, a flood of white
and black which flew past my residence,
as I sat on the porch at my ease, memories
easing their way into my thoughts as rain
fell freely, fluently as the words which I once
shared with abandon with those I loved;
memories and rain rapidly filled
the afternoon, gutters, streets, sidewalks,

and my heart overflowing; past and present
merged; thought, memory, landscape,
and sky a quilt blending inner and outer,
present and past; I slipped into reverie
where all who once mattered visited
and reminded me why they once mattered,
and how I had betrayed all, even those
who have forgiven me; even so, I welcomed

all and we all found smiles and a hope
or two for the future, and then I awoke
to a wet world drying, clouds flown,
and workers cleaning up leaves, sweeping
and mopping water from inconvenient
places; I realized solitude, the soft song
of water dripping from bush and tree,
the whisper of a cooling breeze, and smiled.

Kigali, Rwanda, September 2012

A LIFE

(for John Herzog and David Ellenstein)

the performance ends
and the sadness begins
the slow trek out of the theatre

the body drained
the mind stunned by what
it has once again seen

the heart flutters
against the ribs like a butterfly
about to run out of time

and drift to earth's final embrace
yet tomorrow he will be back
in full magnificent flight above

the audience above his limitations
above the world as he daily lives it
until the virtual reality releases him

once again into the gray streets
which hold him until another day
gives him one more chance to soar

A JOURNEY

Walking down a dirt path in the middle of a city,
I am jolted out of my thoughts by a mini-van
and a motorcycle blasting past me. They swerve

onto the cobblestone road which is my destination.
I stop, breathe deeply, and try to relax as the sound,
dust, and exhaust fumes abate. I find a well

of silence into which I slowly slide. I look down
a long dirt path which glides deep into a valley
where farm fields appear in the midst of the city,

a surprising treasure trove of greenery, order,
and beauty which lies at the bottom of this rutted
track which I am about to abandon. This could be

the story of my adult life: not seeing, taking
the less desirable path repeatedly, ignoring
what literally lies before me. Silence blesses me,

and my breathing becomes slow and peaceful. Gradually,
I realize this silence is filled with birdsong, the hum
of insects, and the distant cries of children at play.

The grace and serenity of these sounds soothe
with the sweeping comfort found in ocean waves
lapping at an empty beach. As my eyes rise up

from the fields below, hills blossom all across
the valley in waves which rise, then fall, then rise
ever higher until the horizon absorbs all beauty

into itself. (This is one of the dangers of my love
of nature. The horizon always is calling. I seem
seldom able to accept the beauty before me, always

wanting more, seeking the unknown, listening
to voices and sounds which I can not quite name
or recognize. I have lived a life in which I have

witnessed great beauty of landscape and person
and event, yet I always want more or different
or better. Whatever that actually means is seldom

clear.) Eventually, I awaken from my reverie
and rejoin the world of people who noisily
populate my journey back home with their

cries of hope and anger and anguish and joy.
Inside my mind, I still see the valley and hills,
and hear the birds and insects and children.

Kigali, Rwanda, September 2012

A FEW WORDS IN PASSING

robes of wind
hair of rain

lips of blossom
smile of flame

dance beneath
a harvest moon

where all are young
but old too soon

remember me when
time has flown

and sing for me
above my stone

Kigali, Rwanda, May 2012

A CEREMONY OF THE RAINY SEASON

All afternoon twisted sheets of rain
rattled the roof, sewed patterns of rivers

and streams on windows and porch,
and rode the wind in exuberant dances,

wind which shook doors, walls, and birds
struggling to stay aloft and birds perched

on limb, bush, and the roof across the street.
Lightning lit the late afternoon near and far,

and thunder rumbled with the guttural sounds
of bass tympani. The dirt road outside

the school grew mounds of mud -- islands
in the streams crisscrossing one another

in a long downhill journey which spanned
the length and breadth of the humble path

trod by young and old, and deeply scarred
by vehicles of every conceivable description.

As evening arrived, the wind eased into a breeze,
clouds drifted off in several directions,

a quarter moon appeared in the gradually
clearing sky, stars grew brighter

and increased in number, and the air
was brisk, clean, and a tonic to the spirits

of all who crept out of homes, stores,
and alleyways to chat, laugh, flirt,

and celebrate the recently baptized cathedral
of sky, street, field, child, man, and woman.
(Kigali, Rwanda, November 2013)

A BRAHMS AFTERNOON

It was a wind-lashed, cloud-strewn, rainy afternoon.
Trees, swaying wildly, moaned their complaints and shed branches.
Thunder's tympani kept up a steady percussive accompaniment
and lightning carved its calligraphy across the ominous sky.

The streets were deserted save for an occasional speeding car
and a very few pedestrians sprinting for cover holding newspapers
or briefcases or even an umbrella or two above their scurrying forms.
I sat near an open window for hours, sipping hot chocolate,

shifting my vision back and forth between the view outside
and a book of poetry by Antonio Machado while listening
to Brahms. Eventually, I fell asleep and dreamed of floating
on rivers where the only visible people populated distant shores

and their voices were falling leaves in wind. When I awoke,
the rain had ceased, life outside was reborn, and night displayed
a thousand or more stars above children splashing in puddles,
old folk out for a stroll, and teenagers populating shadows

with touch and gentle laughter. A cool breeze ruffled curtains
in my living room, and a spaniel stared at me from the sidewalk.
I decided to end the day with a Brandenburg Concerto: elegance,
serenity, and civilized order seemed appropriate to the moment.

Kigali, Rwanda, March 2013

LISTENING TO BEETHOVEN'S NINTH SYMPHONY

Thunder reverberates throughout La Paz.
In sympathetic vibration, the Andes respond.

I turn sixty-three and hear voices
murmuring across the years. Old fears and new

are summoned by the night, the future shrinks,
the past dims, and the moment expands

and diminishes as thunder rises and fades.
All these years and still there are no words

to describe what has been, what is, and what
is to come. The music ends,

as does the storm. Once again I am alone.
Still there is no peace, only the faint melody

of voices past and to come, the quiet
drumming of the heart, and a breeze

lifting and releasing living room curtains.
When rain brushes the window,

I set sail on an ocean of sleep.
Who knows where I will awaken?

(La Paz, Bolivia, October 31, 2008)

RIP THE STRINGS LET FLY THE FEET

fingers dance up and down guitar strings
dresses flip flop and fly up and down calves and thighs
of lasses whirling twirling flying across the floor
lightly attached to hands of swains swirling behind

around and side to side their partners
while a bow hand releases a cascade of notes
wildly exuberantly ecstatically fiddled
the night is aflame with the freedom of Saturday night

tomorrow the sturdy bassist who is the band's foundation
will don his janitor's suit to sweep up the ashes
still hearing the music around him still seeing
bodies flying above the music and the floor

still remembering the little red head who kept
bringing him one cool drink after another

TO BE UNGAINLY IS NO CRIME

Waves rise and fall, steadily flow,
an enactment of thought, hopes, dreams;

would that my body could mirror this shape,
could glide, raise itself, lower itself, spin,

leap, and drift. Alas, whatever gifts were present
when young, these old bones define (in their aged,

inept way) what it is to hobble, lurch, stumble, creak,
and limp, and my mind adopts the same forms far too often.

And yet, and yet, and yet, in my clumsy movements,
my inelegant prose, my cack-handed gestures

designed to create connections, I find a friend or two
discover an idea or phrase here or there of modest use,

and even discover a glimmering of an insight. And thus I learn
to forgive myself (and others) for that which does not delight,

but merely cracks open a door or window, hints, nudges (no matter in
how ungainly a manner), and suggests all is not lost, not shattered.

HEART OF THE NIGHT

The moon and I
at the window;

sighing trees, limbs caressed by the wind,
arch and bend along the road;

stolid witnesses, the mountains
loom above in a solemn silence;

and a brilliant necklace sparkles
in the immense darkness overhead.

If I open the window,
will my life change?

(La Paz, Bolivia, November 25, 2008)

HERE COMES THE RAIN

Soaking wet in afternoon downpour,
a walker's mind floats across years between
childhood's wild sojourns in rain,
(where he played basketball
and football with unfettered
delight and amazement that no one
called him home or scolded him
when he finally returned),
and an old man's perambulations
through wind-blown, rain-drenched streets,
where he is splashed by cars and trucks,
trudges through ankle deep puddles,
and sings to accompaniment of thunder
to his own amazement, (he who is so

terrified of lightning), walking up
a mountainside in the Andes bellowing
verses from an old Spiritual, "Didn't it
rain, Children, Lord didn't it rain;"
walking down a hillside in Kigali belting out
an old Clancy Brothers standard,
"And always remember the longer you live,
the sooner you bloody well die;"
waving to people crouched under trees
and in doorways of small shops.
At times, this seems the best part of his life:
walking, singing, dancing, celebrating
rain, rain, rain, and finding life beyond
the quotidian in a world of water;

he discovers herons, sea gulls, ducks,
loons, egrets, geese, songbirds
huddled on powerlines over a creek,
and now and again, another man
or woman walks past, or pedals past
on a bike, lost in their own wet worlds,
but aware enough to distribute a smile
or casual salute, even, on occasion,
the gift of a few words that acknowledge
a brother or sisterhood unknown to occupants
of vehicles splashing past, miserable driving
in such weather, while these privileged few walk
and pedal with inexplicable joy. These folk
are forever one good storm away from delight.

A FINAL GOODBYE

When the ashes that had been my father,
but were no longer my father
(he who was gone but still
my father),

when the ashes had joined the great circling
of the globe that is the ocean and all its life
and death and time time time that flows
past man's limits, being before and after

what man is,
when the ashes had gone, I was left
with a voice which loved to argue
but had grown silent deprived of its

favorite conversational adversary
who was now molecules rejoining
the great chain of life, the endless flowing
which nurtures all life and joins generations.

Did his courage go with him,
that brave man who looked death in the eye
with an indifference born of the sea,
coming as he did from seafaring stock?

Did his love of over sixty years go with him,
filling the ocean with a passion
which would birth new life
and one final series of questions:

this grief, this constant melancholy, this
inconsolable loss, is it for the ashes afloat
in the ocean, is it for the man who was and is
no more, is it for the woman left alone,

is it merely a selfish song sung as a child's lament
of me me me me me why did you leave me,
as if cancer were a choice and old age avoidable?
Ebb and flow in peace deep within your new home.

THE RINGMASTER DISMISSES ANOTHER

A great, unutterable silence falls
and a family's life-giver
slips on death's dark, unfathomable shawl,
which allows no light, not a sliver.

Each member of the family
recalls different events and images.
Who is to say which recital
bears truth, insight, or triage

for those left standing alone
at night's edge? Which words release
a survivor from a desire to atone,
ensure for self and others some peace?

How many days and nights must pass
before self-loathing at not doing enough slips
from mind, and heart, and sense dives into past
where it meditates on life's curious drift?

For all, sooner or later, this great circus
points us toward the exit. Better, it seems,
to take a bow, turn, and leave without fuss,
yet I find many who've left adrift in my dreams.

RITE OF WIND AND EARTH

leaf floats into open hand
soft landing in midst of windstorm
hand trembles at such grace
such delicacy and mourns

passing of life kneels in yard
places leaf in pile of others
and prays all fallen leaves

with be welcomed by earth
all fallen be welcomed

all life be adorned with meaning

INTOXICATION

Crickets sound in chorus, a stream
more varied than brook water
burbling over mountain rocks.

Stars baptize children
loose in the fields.
The moon pours its light,

thick and rich as honey,
upon lovers abed in grass, arms
wrapped round an imagined future.

An old couple rocking on a porch
listen to cricket, bird, and child's voice
telling all to come safely in;

they dream a canoe on
a long ago lake; they drift
back and forth, back and forth, across time.

MOTH

in lamp light
crazed with unutterable

desire

drawn to immolation
wings sing love love love

HERMANOS

seal sleek and wild
sails above creek
deer bolts from shore brush
border collie barks and races

round nearby yard
startled loons take flight
I sit on big rock creek-side
(in midst of hills trees path

overgrown by blackberry
bushes tangles of vines
tree roots sprouting through earth)
and find myself laughing

boisterously as though I too
were feral unrestrained free

SUMMER BECKONS AND MEMORY SUMMONS

The meadow opens once again:
out tumble honeysuckle, blackberries,
a thousand flowers, baseball, the rituals
of courtship, the freedom of dance,

and the long afternoons flowing down
to the lake or river or sea, whichever
was closest, and the leisurely stroll
into evening and family and dinner,

the night filled with fireflies, falling stars,
and the musical lilt of children's voices
chanting the words of hide and go seek,
the parents listening and watching from porches,

and the slow drifting off to sleep where
the fields were endless and all sounds were music.

THE LAD WITH SPRING IN HIS STEP

A lad came stutter stepping down a side street,
hair aflame in the sun, Scott Joplin in his feet,
voice softly grooving with bursts of scat singing,
melodies and lyrics shifting every minute or so,

his eyes swiveling back and forth from one side
of the street to the other, tracking the spring walks
of young ladies, talking in song to stray cats, dogs,
and cantankerous crows unwilling to move out

of the way of his spirited stroll that found
inevitable paths (without rancor or menace)
through obstacles large and small, greeting all
who crossed his path with a joie de vivre that left

smiles in his wake and sunshine in conversations flowering
as he disappeared round a corner, far up the street.

DECEMBER SURPRISE

tree leaves mambo all evening
with swirling wind

walking outside my feet
turn frisky join leaves and wind

as leaves wind and feet delight
in dance my face foolishly grins

whirling on rain-filled grass suspends
time blends with wind onlookers grin

SELF-PORTRAIT

I am no one,
I am
everyone I have known:
all those voices coming on the wind

from the past, the aching, haunting past,
the faces barely recognizable in browned
and curled photos found tucked in old books,
in crumpled letters scattered among old poems,

and in boxed up bric a brac long forgotten;
who, I ask myself, am I, if not these forgotten ones
who whisper in my head every second of my life,
whose words have shaped thought, deed, laughter,

and hope (that always precious commodity
so easily lost or devalued or mocked or scorned);
to these (sometimes) nameless faces, these
barely audible voices who have shaped and molded

my life, I say welcome and stay as long as I remain,
my mind and heart a decaying dwelling with room
for all who have stretched a hand in my direction,
included me in the casual warmth of a smile, and blessed me

with a simple inquiry as to how life was going; each and every
one of you has left traces woven through my days and hours;
whenever the wind blows at midnight, or the rain curtains off
the outside world, you are there, barely audible, glimpsed

but never fully seen, but always a part of who and what
I have become over these sixty-three years. We are one.
We are a patchwork quilt of friendship, aspiration, and failures
which strengthen our bond. We fill the night with might have been and is.

We are the dreamed, the dreamer, the stranger who became more
and then vanished, the intimate who disappeared into the long night,
but left behind words, images, and the tilt of a head which remain
in memory's ever expanding pouch where nothing is ever completely lost.

March 19, 2009, La Paz, Bolivia

FROM MOMENT TO MOMENT

Each moment is

a poem, complex,
filled with life,

all life's years

distinct, interwoven,
a patchwork quilt

resembling, if we're lucky,

the portrait in the mirror
that we almost recognize

yet always confuses us.

Who am I, the face in the mirror,
or the song in the mind?

Storm at the window, life's confusion,

I welcome you. Chaos provides such
opportunities for discovery.

TO BEAR WITNESS

Motionless on bridge,
I gaze at creek below;

beneath whose surface
an otter swims past,

flips onto its back,
flows back other way.

I would, if I could,
dive deep and swim

parallel to the little creature,
my body a swift song

joining in nature's creation
symphony; but I am no song,

nor can I swim beneath water
for minutes at a time. I am

merely onlooker to world's wild
hymn of creation, never-ending,

never-tiring, a festival beyond kenning,
ever-changing, ever the same.

I gaze upstream, downstream, over
hills and trees, at oncoming storm above.

I was born to see and bear witness.
My task is to record and celebrate.

When rainclouds burst above me, I lift
my face in gratitude to know water

as fish, otter, duck, and loon know water.
Still merely witness, my flesh is consecrated.

LORDS AND LADIES OF THE DANCE

a delight of fingers
jigging across strings
lifting hearts and feet
in rhythmic celebration
of life and its blessings

a voice sails above
a lilting incantation
of what can be
what should be
and we

we float
and bounce
left right left again
turn and spin
we can ride the wind

when the music ends
we wend our way home
sharing golden doubloons
of musical joy as we hum
half-remembered tunes

and skip like children in spring
lah diddly dah hum diddly do
and the rooster crows to greet the dawn
birds lift from trees in great spirals
and a breeze eases our path

IN TUNE

the sound of song in the distance
lifts a heart too concerned with itself

the lilt of a tin whistle
lightens heavy feet

the blur of a reeling fiddle
flings care aside

and a slow air floated by Uilleann pipes
draws to his feet a listener lamed by grief

and reintroduces him to the world
in all its bawdy raucous chaotic aching beauty

LISTENING TO MOUNTAIN MUSIC

I grow old
I weep at archaic fiddle tunes
meant to comfort why why why

frailing banjos make me want
wings to sprout and fly as my feet
struggle to overcome a lack of breath

the dulcimer plants trees in my heart
a wayfaring stranger's home carried within
a bowed psaltery fills the wind

bow down your head and pray
the autoharp commands bow down
wait your fate with serenity

those old wailing voices from the past
crying tales of murder love and broken farms
release my fears and tears why why why

no peace on this broken earth
save within save within
no peace found amid the world's hard times

wrapped in the arms of tunes
instruments and bleeding voices
I rock away the late afternoon...

LIFE AS A FOLK SONG

ho daddy ho
can't jump start the words
locked up tight
garaged in my smoky throat

jenny dang the weaver
who wove my feelings
into this labyrinth
where no light goes

no lark in the morning ever flew
higher than my dreams no wounded bird
dropped into deeper grass than my mind
when hope vanished along a winding road

no orphan train pulled a heavier load
than my feet shuffling through a mountain pass
toward the ocean where waves
would rock me in the cradle of life

just another wayfaring stranger
docking in your harbor loan me
a compass and I'll be on my way
the river be wide and I have days to cross

just a drifting log rolling and bobbing
one day picking some old dance tune
on your banjo you'll look around a corner to see
me knocking splinters loose from your rickety door

we'll find a shady grove and forget these
prodigal years a long time travelling a long time gone
give us a drink of water and let's stretch out
to watch the wind that shakes the barley

GRIEF NOTES

sound of a midnight train
riding an autumn wind

a solo mountain fiddle
mourning its lost forest

a pennywhistle soaring
through a slow Irish air

a tenor sax breathing
the pain of back alleys

lonely bars a red light circling
a three a.m. fallen body

a mother's lullaby while walking
a sick infant all night long

and the hitchhiker humming Woody Guthrie
tunes alone on an empty highway

BARN DANCE

to fiddle away the hours
is there anything finer
    than setting bodies
    a-frenzy with motion

the bow hand dazzles
and bewitches the strings
    a roomful of puppets leap
    and turn tap heel and toe

the strings sing of the world's motion
where time tumbles all in freefall
    and the dancers move faster
    trying to stay on their feet forever

walking home the fiddler skips
a step or two to tunes only he can hear
    the underbrush beside the road teems
    with bounding rabbit and gliding deer

SING THROUGH THE NIGHT

All words vanish
        lightning and wind
all hope follows
        a gray day's loss
                why not sing why
                not sing through the night

Rain floods the land
        and she she and she have drifted away
currently I sit alone
        a gray day's loss
                why not sing why
                not sing through the night

Family is an ocean
        away away oceans away
waving I sit staring blindly
        a gray day's loss
                why not sing why
                not sing through the night

Call for the fiddle
        rosin up the bow
the cello hums a low tune denying
        a gray day's loss
                why not sing why
                not sing through the night

Let musicians I have known (Joseph Daniel
        Vitali Gyorgi Dominic Paulette)
with guitar cello viola piano and tin whistle erase
        a gray day's loss
                why not sing why
                not sing through the night

One rainy evening lost and alone
in one small unnumbered dwelling
let music triumph over
a gray day's loss
why not sing why
not sing through the night

(Cairo, Egypt, December 2001)

LIFT YOUR VOICE AND RAISE YOUR GLASS

(For Colin Chant)

And have you never sung the night through,
sought the note of hope, lost
your voice, your mind, your sense
of time in full-throated pursuit of one moment
to soar soar soar
and forget those years spilled behind
ash ash piles of ash

and did you find did you did you
blind and deaf to all but the one lifting lilting dazzling
eternal note of hope
find a long measureless sound to ride?

POET'S PRAYER

(listening to Beethoven's Ninth Symphony)

to follow a path anywhere it winds,
to feel wind loosen desire, never to tire
riding night, all its might surging

before a final swoop into the depths
of dream, a dazzling drop:

all song ceases, ceases all sound, sound
deceased and feet walk the earth once more (breeze
brushing sand) and my hands know once more
your face   your face   your face

NEITHER ELEGY NOR HYMN

The withered figure bends over the guitar
his fingers subtle as goose feathers
coax melody from his ancient strings
a sound like the wind through falling leaves
or a distant crowd murmuring beyond a hill

His whole life rises round him
Sarah who shared sixty years but now is dust on a breeze
his estranged son buried in a field in Southeast Asia
a daughter who finds it embarrassing to call him father
no one left alive who calls him by his first name

His body enwraps the guitar as though it were a weeping child
imagine dolor given shape and you see him
parchment is less brittle than his skin
the ocean less fluid than his tune
do you hear its steady weeping a lullaby perhaps or incantation

SONGBIRD

a blues note broken in the middle

the songbird in the brambles startled
into silence   shame for the intrusion

all autumn I have wandered in search
of a music which would still this dull grief
for every person I see wandering alone

every child I see looking at the world
with a question unanswered question
every animal abandoned to wander
through traffic in search of death

every couple I see waving arms in
the cursing dance common among
the intimate at war their lips forming
phrases only they know to use
only they can die from only they can still

all autumn music has drifted from alleyways
when I follow there is no one and no sound
music has wafted from waterfronts when I arrive
there is only the rasp of a ferry's horn through fog
music chuckles like a brook or stream from playgrounds
all I find are merry-go-rounds and swings in slow motion

and then the sound of a bird in full throat wild as Sonny Terry
whooping it up and blowing his blues harp to save life in praise
of life to be life and the bird stops me dead in my tracks
and I feel grief flowing out through my arms my feet begin to dance
I move faster I begin to run I am sprinting I am the wind
in search of this blessed sound this freedom this wisdom
this hope and I begin to shout   and in mid-note the song stops...

what song
what song is this
what song is this so sad
what song is this so sad it cheers
what song is this so sad it cheers and vanishes
who is this person so foolish he sits and waits for hours hoping
who sits and waits and begins to sing feathers growing beak forming
who hides in brambles to pour out lamentations easing a world's fatigue...

A DAY WITHOUT MUSIC

How many of these before
unslaked thirst dries mind and soul
irrevocably, leaving victim blind to all
that is worth seeing or doing, unaware
of any idea, creature, or thing which is
moist with hope or belief or love, deaf
to Beethoven's majesty, Bach and Mozart's
elegance, Coltrane's questing heart, in short,
drained of color, flesh, blood, a shadow drifting
silently past the symphonies of everyday life?

IT WAS ALL ABOUT SAX

when man said the wind man
blowing when does the wind do
its voodoo upon leaf and bud

bloody the morning the storm
warning it is on its way its windy
winding wickedly roaring crack

thunder and snap way paving
the air for torrents for sheets waving
water across a landscape bare of movement

save the inexorable march of water
from hill crest to plains vanishing point
he blew harder his sax pumping sound and air

through the fair lands deluged with storm
with the wicked humor of broken notes rediscovered
in new keys the keys of life the keys of change

the keys to who and what I am you may be
maybe the keys to the kingdom of lusty life
he blew and vanished into the club's walls

and everyone left storming through the night
storming to the tunes reverberating in their heads
headed for home and a stormy night in a minor key

REVERIE

(for Joseph Glaser)

I remember his slight figure
bent over his guitar

coaxing the strings
to sing of love and loss and hope

when applause filled the room
he looked up with a shy smile

seemed surprised to find
us in the room

his ending bow was authentic
as a handshake between friends

who have been long separated
and are overjoyed at their reunion

when applause died away
before conversation began

there was a moment when the room
held one remembered note

a struck string summoning the sound
of a bird's wings in flight toward a forest

THE PLAYER

(for Joseph Glaser)

A breeze-curved willow, he bends
over his guitar, feeds the wind

notes, a steady stream of sound.
He is the shaper and the shaped.

His fingers transmute wires into
singing air, bruises into blues.

The carved wood he enfolds
unleashes mind and heart into sound.

When the last note melts to silence,
ears strain, a futile remembrance.

Ah, the music-bereft air,
a desert swiftly grows there.

THERE YOU ARE AGAIN

Wind ransacks trees and bushes
up and down a hillside,
its voice a deep-throated moan
reflecting all mankind's sorrow that betides,

such grief as resides
in cello or oboe,
abandoned child
or grieving widow;

ah, to know a song to sing
that brings peace to all things,
chant it into a suffering world
so majestic hope might be unfurled;

although in truth I would gladly accept
any comfort, no matter how inept.

ALONE ON A NIGHT STREET

Sailing through a midnight sky,
entangled in pine branches,
a golden full moon graces
the night with a beauty

comparable to a Bill Evans
or Duke Ellington solo,
nothing needed to expand
the floating vision;

the world is subtle, and repays
serious contemplation,
a lovely peace stripped
of life's angst and anger;

the simple act of breathing
in and out is a form of prayer.

PRIVACY AT LAST

The stubborn ringing of the doorbell:
it can be no one I know as no one I know
knows where I live,
but the sound persists; it grows louder
like a swarm of angry hornets,

and the phone joins in, as though
it were a referee calling a foul
on my failure to act, to speak, to open
the door to whoever thinks I owe them
my time, my energy, my thought,

my tolerance for whatever they bring.
At last silence, and I return to my late
breakfast which is now cold, less inviting
than I was to whatever strangers were
demanding my attention at door and on phone.

I lean back in my chair, headsets in place so no one
will know of my presence and slip into dream
listening to the pianistic elegance of Duke Ellington,
a most welcome stranger who brings beauty minus
the demands of anything other than quiet pleasure.

IT WAS ALL SAX

arms of night enveloped me
pure sax singing in my ears
heart and caressing my mind
jazz all night long slow jazz
hot jazz dancing jazz and jazz

that slumbered that raised
and lowered blood pressure
love incarnate sweeping me
through long hours of darkness
all was sax sax sax and more sax

when day arrived and all grew still
and silent I rose to face a day
where roses grew and blossomed
everywhere I went and music
whispered at the back of my mind

DOWN HOME MUSICAL COOKING

Tuba Skinny unleashes a bouncing rollicking sound:
cornet, clarinet, trombone, and tuba let sail an ocean
of sound backed by bass, drums, guitar, and washboard

while Erika Lewis wails on vocals, "I Get the Blues,
Sweet Baby." The outdoor audience hollers their approval --

the whole group got that swing, lets loose everything
in heart and mind. If your feet don't dance to this music,
they are surely missing from the end of your legs.

These Dixie blues are sassy, wild, free, and make
a morose man smile, shake his body in testimony to life;

it all comes down to time and sound freed from shackles.
All is knitted together by the wailing frail who sets
the stage on fire and draws the audience into the flames.

Down home cooking, there is nothing quite like it,
whether over a stove, or in a bluesy Dixieland jam.

HOTTER THAN A NEW ORLEANS SUMMER AFTERNOON

all the music is so sweet that feet
all the feet on the street turn fleet
gliding striding and leaping to the beat
proposed by the hot lips and fingertips
of Tuba Skinny winging its way

through Rosa Lee Rosa Lee or any other
tune it chooses to play sometimes
an old hound lies at feet of tuba man
scratching his ears in time to the oompah
bass line some folk dance past on way

to store or restaurant or something perhaps
more personal other dancers become part
of the show sober faces of red hot musicians
now and again crack a smile as free and wild
as music winging from mind heart horns strings

drum washboard voices and imagination
of this band filling a street corner with life
and hope and the unfettered seeming chaos
that somehow blends into a musical gumbo
perfectly seasoned and each player attuned

to the others swept up in a world of their own
oh cornet trombone clarinet and saxophone wail
sail through afternoon skies and streets oh banjo
guitar tuba bass drum washboard strum thrum
be the heartbeat that ties horns to human flesh

ah to be lost in the streets of New Orleans come upon
Tuba Skinny treating a neighborhood to music both
pagan and sacramental wringing hosannas from lips
and swirling feral sensuous untamed dances from shoulders
hips knees feet how sweet that would be with joy how replete

BACK ON THE STREET AGAIN

Tuba Skinny wails; its sound flies up
and down the streets of New Orleans;
passersby find themselves dancing
with abandon; they forget where

they were headed, as they grow
ever more intoxicated by cornet,
clarinet, trombone, guitar, banjo,
tuba, washboard, and a singer

who seems to have time traveled
from the twenties; hey man,
hey woman, stop and listen;
life soars in these musical precincts;

even the wind blows with a Dixieland
rhythm, papers lift off the ground, swoop,
soar, and jitterbug down the street;
the whole world has decided to flip,

flop, and fly, and this ain't no jive --
life is a dance, as long as Tuba Skinny's
music entrances the passing world;
whoa, daddy, whoa mama, let your feet

fly, your heart sing, joy can
be found in everything.

(for my favorite Dixieland street band)

DON'T FRET

Let's spend the night
sliding, gliding, striding
cross the floor.

Don't fret. The bass man
won't let our feet go astray.
Dip, swirl, and sway,

don't let this night get away
without a wild celebration
filled with ecstatic play

of body: legs, hips, chest,
feet, all awhirl, a-twirl,
all combine imagination

with rules of dance, and
liberation of music unleashing
wild hearts in courtship,

in dazzling exploration of time,
space, touch, arriving as one
at a perfect ending.

ADRIFT IN EVENING

twilight fades with grace and elegance
of muted trumpet solo's last notes

drifting into memory   for example
the evanescent sorrow of notes
blown by Miles Davis using a Harmon

mute where the final sounds are
a mere whisper yet contain a lifetime

of grief hope and wistful surmise
so too evening's last wisps of light
contain long departed ocean voyages

athletic and academic feats now
barely credible and vanished lovers

a hint of their smiles the sound
of their voices in night's solitude
caught in last echoes of birdsong

and the lost beauty left behind by Clark Terry
Dizzy Gillespie and Miles always Miles Davis

FINGER POPPING AND TOE TAPPING AT MIDNIGHT

The midnight train is playing its horn again,
jazz for the few visible stars and the man

alone on a shaky balcony which shivers
like a dancer cutting a rug to a swinging

jazz band; the horn fades into the distance
followed by the rambling percussion of wheels

on tracks steadily laying a foundation
for the horn's floating on down the road riffs;

and the man on the balcony rocks back
and forth on an old chair useless to anyone

but the rocker; rain, which had vanished
for a time, resumes and shares its own peculiar

rhythms shaped by a wind which comes
and goes while the old man taps his toes

in a funky counterpoint; all this happens
while a town mostly sleeps under a wet

swirling blanket of wind and rain disturbed only
by the occasional trombone wail of sleepless dogs;

eventually even the old man trundles inside
to find the rhythms of sleep sleep sleep.

AS DAY ENDS

Clark Terry's horn unleashes
a silvery note
                    that ascends
                              ever higher
                                        to join a golden full moon
                                                  rising into early evening orbit.

When the note ends, listeners
discover they have forgotten
                    to breathe,
                              and slowly rejoin
                                                  their quiet neighborhood

and prepare for sleep
          where they will drift
down a midnight river filled
          with remembrance of music
and the unspooling of life.

AND THEN THERE WERE NONE

Old man on a balcony
rocked his grief through
long afternoon, listened

to *Sketches of Spain*
hour upon hour, smoked
a pipe redolent of cloves,

an empty rocker next
to his draped with flowery
cushions, rocking from time

to time when wind chimed in.
He hummed trumpet solos
in broken raspy voice, recited lines

from King Lear with quiet passion
of Miles Davis or Bill Evans
at their melancholy best,

"O, thou'lt come no more.
Never never never never never."
He fell asleep while the music

played on, caught in a loop.
Miles welcomed onset of dusk.
Night spread its inevitable blanket.

TWO WHO HAVE SEEN BETTER DAYS

Exuberant rain dances on a spring window
in concert with Ramsey Lewis unleashing
"Hang on Sloopy" on the radio;

who would have thought it possible
piano, rain, and wind might lift an old man
to his feet in an aging parody of a jig;

the septuagenarian's ragged voice belts out
those words that can be remembered while
the visitor in the room, an old friend unseen

for years, sings along, misses as many words
as his host in a wild unanticipated toast to life;
neither of these old scoundrels are fit to dance,

much less sing, but both give it all they got, as wind
rises and falls, as rain sweeps away lost and lonely years,
as life flowers in the most unlikely of crucibles.

AN EVENING JOURNEY

In early evening hush,
rain's soft susurration,
with a quiet elegance
one might find in a Bill Evans
or Lester Young or Miles Davis
solo, flows through open windows,
carries me from contemplation
into deep sleep where I float

downhill riding creek's current
through forests, past boulders,
into meadows where voices
of children echo, and distant past
welcomes me without question,
as certain songs or tunes
stir the heart whenever they
are sung or played,

such as "God Bless the Child,"
"Summertime," or "Stella by Starlight,"
and I drift through waves of music,
and the world laps against
my mind as it dozes, just as I drift
in and out of consciousness
when the rain carries me into memory,
then back to the edges of today.

JUST OUT FOR A WALK
(for Joseph Glaser and Robert Fox)

downtown small town backstreets
gimping along, walking stick in hand,
my feet beat the street like a drummer

always just behind the beat and all
around me folk create their own music
an old woman on a corner scolding

herself in staccato bursts of sound
Coltrane would have recognized
three wee bairns skip rope and chant

in rhythms Horace Silver might
have included in his best work
a lad bops swiftly through a nearby

intersection with the funky
lightning quick deftness of the mighty
Charlie Parker dancing through a solo

his groove moving at the speed of light
leaning against a wall with the weight
of years and the world two old men

quietly talk talk and talk mixing smiles
and soulful nods as they shake heads
at all they've seen and known both

kind of blue conversation sailing
wherever memory and imagination
take them sharing riffs that fit

together with the perfection
of Miles musically chatting
with Cannonball and Trane

and I suddenly realize all life
is music harmonious dissonant
free-flowing stuttering full-throated

whispered celebratory or grief-stricken
all contain melody rhythm (heart)beat
memory and imagination

THEY ALL INHABIT THE NIGHT

all night I dreamed I was lost
at sea in an alley on a battlefield
in a junkyard in a waterfront dive

when suddenly I found a room
filled with music where fear
was eased where losses were mourned

where hope was discovered where
horns and voices and rippling piano
blessed all who listened as a rainstorm

washed streets and buildings as lightning
flashed and thunder roared and music
blended in perfect harmony and suddenly

I recognized those who filled my dream
oh Ella whose scat singing sweeps away
all pain ah Lady Day who absorbs all grief

in your broken voice while Lester's sax
soothes your heartbreak damn my eyes
and ears Coleman's raw power matches

Joe Williams' unfettered exuberance
note for note and the mighty Miles Trane
Cannonball collaboration makes a dreamer

kind of blue and thoroughly blessed
while Dizzy and Bird reinvent
music's possibilities and I sing along

in my dream with wild abandon
pure sound with no words needed
until I wake with song fading

from my head yet buried in my heart
heirlooms of music I will never lose
as long as their magic names resound

NEWS COMES OF YOUR DEMISE

(for Ben Saltman, 1927-1999)

A picture, a poem, a book,
a few anecdotes, a foolish
argument barely remembered,

a dinner where we saved
the world from fools
much like us, these few

things are all I carry with me,
and I grieve that so little
remains of one who meant

so much for so long;
in restaurant where I sit
staring at your wife's letter,

an old jukebox plays "So What"
from *Kind of Blue*, in a room filled
with expats from a dozen nations,

and I remember our discussions
of relative merits of Miles versus
Trane, Ellington versus Basie,

Lady Day versus Ella,
and all those thousands of words
now seem inane; only the music matters,

as only the life mattered;
I pray we did not waste both,
and the music continues to fill

the small cafe in Tashkent
where I grieve, thousands of miles
and a dozen years from home.

Dolor fills the horns of Trane,
Miles, and Cannonball, music that mourns
life's limitations yet eases my distress.

I sip a Benedictine and Brandy, eavesdrop
on conversations in multiple languages,
understand nothing but irreparable loss.

(Tashkent, Uzbekistan, 1999)

WHISPERS OF THE HEART

My mother, voice colored by the hint of Virginia
even after decades away, softly talks of years past,
friends, parents, deceased spouse, siblings,
all lost to mortal frailty, swallowed by time.

Her monologue has the gentle beauty of a solo
by Bill Evans at his most introspective. His musings
deftly drawn on a keyboard and her murmurs
to listening sons are as one, quiet music that soars.

It sometimes seems that all life, whether muted or lived
with abandon, is an elegy for time's relentless movement,
whether past, present, or future. No matter how restrained
or uninhibited, life expresses whispers of the heart.

AIN'T IT THE TRUTH

choirs of insects serenade night
couples bury faces in lovers' hair
distant train's cry soars through dark
town settles into silence
one face peers through half-opened window
seeking a single light

as Mose Allison sings in the background
"Your mind is on vacation, but your mouth
is working overtime"
story of my life thinks the listener
wishing there was someone available
to share his "overtime"

Allison launches into
"Seventh Son of a Seventh Son"
auditor mutters I should be so lucky
trashes his whiskey bottle
collapses on the couch
slips into muted snores

FRIDAY NIGHT DELIGHT

Twang of a bottleneck guitar sings into neon night;
swings bodies aching to dance up, down, and around,
time after time after time in a whirling world where bodies

rhyme; legs glued to legs, hips to hips, and lips to lips;
guitar's ringing invitation to take flight lingers in heavy
humidity like a final sip of sweet, bitter lemonade enticing

drinker to take one more taste, just one; and a crazy pianist
blazes up and down a keyboard, an alto sax sets fire
to the heavy air in the crammed club with sawdust

covering the floor, just one dropped match away
from a conflagration, a word that captures the blues
trio who ignite every person in the joint into a burning,

blazing mass that jumps, jives, and dives with wild
uninhibited movement, movement one step away from collapse,
from making love, from taking flight into a new world and time.

OF FIREFLIES JAZZ AND LOST RELATIVES

In the gloaming's last embers, a swirl of fireflies
flits, flashing brief bursts of light, as certain
trumpet and sax players will play swift staccato
notes, each one perfect, lighting the minds,
imaginations, and hearts of listeners who
have no idea how such perfection is achieved,

knowing only that life will never be this perfect
again, just as the children chasing the fireflies
will never again be so filled with joy, as this
moment when time stops and all is wild surmise
about this moment and the next and the next;
the perfection of visual and sonic beauty remains

forever beyond understanding, no matter how many
tomes seek to explain; yet heart, mind, memory,
and imagination embrace both with the fervor
with which we cling to the debris left by a departed parent.
Somehow when I remember fireflies, departed musical
geniuses, and vanished friends and relatives, I hear

the anguished beauty of Miles Davis navigating the heartrending
currents of Concierto de Aranjuez, as fireflies navigate
evening breezes, as great horn players fly, float, and dance
with ease through difficult passages, and we, one and all,
are blown here and there, always seeking beauty and its
ineffable pain, peace, and liberation from self.

BOIL'EM CABBAGE DOWN

Mark O'Connor and Wynton Marsalis erupt into a mighty sound
on fiddle and trumpet dancing round their musical playground
with a red hot band helping to boil'em cabbage down;

the tune leaps from fingers and lips with a red hot flame;
the notes have wings flying round the stage, every musician
engaged in a frenzy celebrating life with a gusto that flows

from trumpet, whirls from fiddle strings, is driven by rock steady
bass keeping their world in sync while a sax rips along beneath it all;
rhythm guitar, drums, and piano ripple and swirl

through whatever musical gullies need filling; every face is lit
with the purest joy, the audience claps and shouts, and their world
is intoxicated for six or seven minutes of musical frenzy;

when it ends, applause builds, everyone is standing, and all
know they have been blessed in ways that can't be anticipated.
Leaving, feet bounce on springs of remembered musical joy.

SUDDENLY ON A BACKSTREET

A trumpet from a nearby building soars
with wild brilliance of tone, swoops
down, down, down into lowest reaches
of its range, dances higher once again
in a playful pattern of two steps higher,

one lower, two more up the staircase,
then veers into wild leaps, bounding
throughout the range of trumpet
possibilities, the tone pure, harsh,
guttural, celebratory, grieving,

notes slow, soft, barely audible, then
blaring, rising higher and higher with unfettered
volume and passion; finally, the music
stops mid-note; looking up, I discover a man
of indeterminate age in a ragged plaid shirt,

horn in hand, in a window three stories
above me, eyes lost in the distance, face pressed
against panes, wearing an expression of loss,
as he watches a troupe of lads shouting
and laughing in a celebration of youth's freedom.

As I walk away, I hear the tears of a Harmon mute,
barely audible, whispering "Round Midnight."
I glance behind me to discover the trumpeter
has opened his window to bestow his song
upon barren streets as shadows envelop his world.

IN A DOWNTOWN DANCEHALL

Rollicking, rocking, roaring denizens of the dance floor
freestyle wild flips, turns, leaps, splits, astonishing
feats of ingenuity that shape movement sans limitation,
as some long forgotten swing band blazes over the speakers,
and those on the sidelines shout encouragement
and occasional suggestions; feet glide, slide, skip, boot,
scoot, and boogie all round the hall; arms wave overhead,
drop down to sides as fingers wiggle, hips swing and sway,
and all of day's worries and confusion slips away
in the holy fury of bodies liberated in exuberant exploration
of space, time, movement, and unfettered imagination.

JOYOUS EVENING WITH THE BLUES

Dexter Gordon blew blue
blue notes for hours in his visit
to my CD player,

accompanied by wicked syncopations
rapped on window and roof
by bursts of rain as it came and went

and returned again, as Mr. Gordon
and the Junior Mance Trio entranced
Montreux back in 1970, along

with me and my two friends
silently nodding in (more or less) time
to music from over forty-five years ago

and icy rain in the here and now;
we spent time consuming "Fried Bananas,"
dreaming of a "Sophisticated Lady,"

bouncing and dancing in chairs and on sofa
to "Rhythm-a-Ning," slow swaying
to "Body and Soul," tears in our eyes,

rediscovering the essence of the blues
in "Blue Monk," and bopping out
freely and wildly around the room

in response to "The Panther."
When the CD concert ended, we all
smiled and silently went our various ways,

and the rain continued a slow serenade,
as if it too had been taken on a journey
that led to a joyous copious weeping.

A WORLD OF HER OWN

A churning of notes, a riptide
of furious sound, saxophonist
in full flight through night air;

passersby swing and sway
moving on down the sidewalk
past the young woman, face scrunched

as she unleashes volleys of notes
into cool night air, hot notes heating
a swirl of shoppers, clubbers,

looky loos, young lovers, the too cool
and too hip, the casual and the solemn,
the straight and the weird, the loud

and the silent, the alert and the aloof --
a Saturday night ocean of people
breaking around the rippling island

world created by the woman and her
wildly whirling body and saxophone
whittling a musical sculpture only she

can fully see, fully hear, fully fathom,
yet prompting stutter steps and wild
swirling passages by half attentive

passersby on their way to god knows where,
every person in his or her own world,
but all touched or brushed or briefly moved

by the intense musician who ignores
one and all on their passages to nowhere
as she finds salvation in a red hot horn.

VINTAGE INN, ASHLAND, OREGON (4/16/81)
(for The PJQ Quintet)

Trumpet and Voice roam together
Sax gusts above
Piano Keys
spill and tumble (a mountain creek
or lover filled with abandon)   Love Her   raps Drum

ice cubes swing
rattle
sway
floorboards dance
CRAZY
a cartoon

every marriage needs witnesses and we nod
clap our hands   stomp our feet   such noisy guests
a wonder we're allowed to stay

silence tightens breathing
we wonder if more's to come...

tipping the waiter we imagine
a collection for lovers
and grin foolishly

outside the night is filled
with cigarette smoke   lightning
and Lithia Creek swirling over rocks
and wooden supports of the Vintage Inn

we sit on our car's hood for hours
with friends
we pretend
we're a traveling band   our hands
shape imaginary notes

ah love love crazy love   nothing quite like it
for igniting the blood   you and I are muted trumpet
softly singing of night and day   swirling sax celebrating
what is and is to come   sensuous guitar and rippling piano
all suggestive of what could be   all suggesting the night
is ours   and the wind whispers of the hours to come

HARRY INSPIRED BY THE PRESERVATION HALL JAZZ BAND

rattlin' bones rattlin' bones just the cost an old man pays
dancin' round his livin' room tryin' to enjoy life alone
but full of zest ripplin' with vim vigor and hot sauce fuelin'
feet ziggin' and zaggin' the blinds closed to the outside
but inside the old guy bip bop boogies all evenin'
scat singin' to old jazz tunes feelin' in them old bones
rattle rattle rattle we still got it sing the bones as feet bounce
flip flop and fly off the wall off the ceiling off the floor
into a wild bebopalooza welcome time may be fleetin'
but this moment can last forever in its inimitable whirlin' swirl
back and forth up and down and when the old dude collapses
on his couch he is laughin' laughin' wailin' like a human trombone

LIVING THE BLUES

Her voice shredded, turned to gravel
by cigarettes and whiskey, she navigates
grocery aisles and checkout lines

as sotto voce she sings old songs
both jazz and country. People stare
in amazement as her ruined voice

elicits tears from listening bystanders.
In her living room she croons with records
of Billy Holiday, Peggy Lee, and Patsy Cline.

If you ask her, she will tell you that she used
to sing in bars and an occasional night club,
but no one will hire her any more

because she got into too damned many fights
with customers, bartenders, and piano players.
Damn the booze she will mutter, but then

she'll tell any listener that she loves whiskey
better than any man, any place, anything
except music. And she will launch into

an old blues tune from the thirties
and slow dance round the room, glass
in hand, oblivious to one and all.

A JAZZ THANKSGIVING OF A SORT

It was a rainy Thanksgiving when
everyone I was related to
or knew even somewhat
were out of town.

I found some semi-edible
turkey at Hughes Market, along
with frozen stuffing that proved
reasonably tasty, adequate

pumpkin pie slices, and discovered
leftover corn bread in my refrigerator.
I fumbled through jazz LPs and 45s in
a bin stashed against a wall and found

solace for a mournful afternoon: First,
Song for My Father. a fine upbeat
album by Horace Silver that led me
to beat my feet and play a drumbeat

on my dining room table while filling
my mouth with second hand food
from the supermarket; "Hang on Sloopy,"
the Ramsey Lewis jazz version of a pop hit,

had me bopping my head and scat singing
in my clumsy fashion; then Oscar Brown, Junior,
launched into his version of Nat Adderley's
"Work Song," and I was on my feet, singing along

at the top of my voice (not a problem as my
neighbors were all out of town), dancing,
stuffing my mouth with pumpkin pie, downing
rum and coke, and worrying my mutt, who found

a corner to curl up in. Some leftover turkey brought
her out of hiding. I put on Lou Rawls singing,
"Stormy Monday," just as the storm outside unleashed
lightning, thunder, and a wild windblown burst

of rain that shook the apartment. The timing made me
laugh and sing in harmony (of a sort) with Lou Rawls.
I picked up the little mutt and danced her around the room.
She tolerated the dance, as long as I fed her more scraps.

When I put her down, she retreated to her corner. I
finished my dinner serenade by playing a duet between
Ben Webster and Coleman Hawkins which led me to the couch
where I fell asleep, a pleasant ending to a solo Thanksgiving.

When I awoke, the wind was playing storm riffs outside my window,
rain was drumming on the building, and I embraced the darkness
with a grin, and a mumbled prayer of Thanksgiving. My hound climbed
onto the couch and curled up at my feet. My day was complete.

AT A WINDOW

Snow was falling, winding
sheets in Amman's dusk,
years spiraling past.

Miles 'round midnight
blew blue notes
each cooler than the snow.

No cold, there was no cold like memory,
frozen on a windowsill, the liquid
of her voice embalmed.

Notes cracked, ice
ready for a thaw,
the wind hinting at life's losses.

Heaters rumbled bass notes,
the shutters shivered in irregular rhythm,
the horn held it all together, a winter psalm.

Amman, Jordan, December 1992

PASSION FLOWER

After The Duke's quietly rippling, opening statement, such passion
in that flower as it opens to a world of unsuspecting listeners,
and Johnny Hodges sings in purest of alto sax voices a long limpid line,

elegantly phrased, a lovely horn grown flower of ineffable beauty
rising inevitably to bluest of deep blue skies, a musical flower
bestowing benediction on all within hearing, casually bequeathed,

with a look that suggests you don't truly understand what you are
being given, and the tone soars, then whispers, always pure, always
silky, always creamy, and the world for a few minutes grows more

beautiful, listeners float in a river of perfection, then all who hear
are diminished as all becomes once again ordinary, as the last perfect
note drops into silence, and Hodges disappears from behind the microphone,

and all is silence, all is routine, the quotidian coats life with blandness,
and all who heard the musical marvel that was Johnny Hodges play, pray
that memory will retain what was heard and bear witness that beauty can exist.

MAKING MY PEACE

Leaves and grass gleamed so brightly
in the rain slanting from the west
merging with the sun's setting rays

that I saw miniature reflections
of my life's history all the way
back to sliding down the birth canal,

the rain and sun a harp and muted trumpet
in a sad yet frisky dance
as trees hummed in witness.

I looked up and saw my future--
the shriveling to dust, the riding of wind, the flowering
bush on the grave where birds nest, a sweet rural shade.

REDEMPTION COMES IN MANY FORMS

in my head I carry
a lifetime of images

Andean rock faces
dotted with occasional shrubbery

late afternoon sun spreading
a golden carpet across rippling Pacific

fishermen quietly at work in the middle
of a mountain lake as sun slowly rises

rolling green hills of Kigali beneath
evening lightning and rumbling thunder

a surfer poised seemingly forever on a wave
about to break upon a Santa Monica beach

deer floating through a Washington forest
before vanishing in dawn mist

an owl majestically lit by late afternoon
sun spilling through dappled branches and leaves

and the face of every woman man or child
who has been kind in my times of need

STRIPPED OF ALL BUT ESSENCE

There was a woman
whose beauty set leaf
and bush aflame
wherever she passed.

When she grew old, she sat
in a rocker beneath a silver moon
which painted her grave face
with the austere loveliness

of life lived fully and pain known
and absorbed into bone and sinew.
All who saw her wanted to stare,
but glanced away in fear of, and longing

for, such elegance and sorrow blended
into a face stripped of all but essence.

JUST ANOTHER FOLK TALE

There are friends who wandered down an unmarked highway
and disappeared into fog. Their silence lasted for years. When they
reappeared, their voices whispered only grief notes shaping tales no one

chose to believe for such things could not be. No one could know
such sorrow and live. Why should we believe in what we heard, save

for the frail beauty of the survivors that shone from their eyes and cheek bones,
and the deep dolor they exhaled with every breath, every word, every step.
Where they passed, silence followed, and people turned back to the arms

of family, and uttered silent thanks they lived lives devoid of such operatic
scope, such bold and overwhelming color. The old friends drifted like clouds

into forest, stream, mountain, and sea. This time they did not return,
but on certain stormy nights I swear by all I hold sacred I hear them
calling me to take a chance, step out into the unknown, risk all.

THE GUITARIST HAS PLAYED FOR HOURS

(for Joseph Glaser)

No one is listening. The lasagna is too good,
the fat man soaked in burgundy is too loud,
there are too many jewels, too much perfume.
too many negotiations going on, yet the small

figure curved round the guitar
plays with delicacy and passion, humming
to himself, lightly tapping his foot, smiling
when Dowland, Tansman, or Rodrigo elegantly emerges.

A vine-wrapped arbor has grown round the small stage
and birds whistle an accompaniment. The space
floods with whirling shadows in antique dress. What better
refuge from life's commerce, he thinks, than music?

Ah, to soar musically as a porpoise dances on air, a dancer
glides across a stage, to achieve the sublime, a state of grace.

BIOGRAPHY

Michael L. Newell was born in Florida in 1945. In addition to living in thirteen states, he has lived in Japan, The Philippine Islands, Thailand, The United Arab Emirates, Jordan, Kuwait, Uzbekistan, Mexico, Egypt, Estonia, Saudi Arabia, Bolivia, and Rwanda. He currently lives in a small town on the Florida coast.

Newell studied writing with Benjamin Saltman and Ann Stanford. His poems have appeared in a number of periodicals including *Aethlon: The Journal of Sport Literature*; *Bellowing Ark*; *College English*; *Current*; *English Journal*; *First Class*; *The Iconoclast*; *Issa's Untidy Hut, Jerry Jazz Musician*; *Lilliput Review*; *Poetry Depth Quarterly*; *Rattle*; *Shemom*, *Ship of Fools*; *Tulane Review*; and *Verse-Virtual.*

Some of his previous books include *A Stranger to the Land*; *Seeking Shelter*; *A Long Time Traveling*; *Traveling without Compass or Map*, *Meditation of an Old Man Standing on a Bridge*; *Wandering*; and *Each Step a Discovery.*

ISBN: 978-81-8253-739-2

First Edition: 2021
Rs. 200/-

Cyberwit.net
HIG 45 Kaushambi Kunj, Kalindipuram
Allahabad - 211011 (U.P.) India
http://www.cyberwit.net
Tel: +(91) 9415091004
E-mail: info@cyberwit.net

Printed at VCORE CONNECT LLP.

www.ingramcontent.com/pod-product-compliance
Lightning Source LLC
Chambersburg PA
CBHW031522180726
48282CB00056B/213
* 9 7 8 8 1 8 2 5 3 7 3 9 2 *